The Choctaw Nation

by Allison Lassieur

Consultant:
Judy Allen
Executive Director of Public Relations
Choctaw Nation of Oklahoma

Bridgestone Books
an imprint of Capstone Press
Mankato, Minnesota

Bridgestone Books are published by Capstone Press
151 Good Counsel Drive, P.O. Box 669, Mankato, Minnesota 56002
http://www.capstone-press.com

Library of Congress Cataloging-in-Publication Data
Lassieur, Allison.
   The Choctaw nation/by Allison Lassieur.
   p. cm.—(Native peoples)
   Includes bibliographical references and index.
   ISBN 0-7368-0832-9
   1. Choctaw Indians—Juvenile literature. [1. Choctaw Indians. 2. Indians of North
America—Southern States.] I. Title. II. Series.
E99.C8 L28 2001
973'.04973—dc21
                                                                  00-009819

Summary: An overview of the past and present lives of the Choctaw, including their
history, food and clothing, homes and family life, religion, and government.

Editorial Credits
Rebecca Glaser, editor; Karen Risch, product planning editor; Timothy Halldin, cover
   designer; Heather Kindseth, production designer; Linda Clavel, illustrator; Heidi Schoof,
   photo researcher

Photo Credits
Judy Allen, cover, 6, 8, 12, 16, 20
Kenneth H. Carleton, 18
Lisa Reed, 14
Vonna Loper, 10

1 2 3 4 5 6 06 05 04 03 02 01

Table of Contents

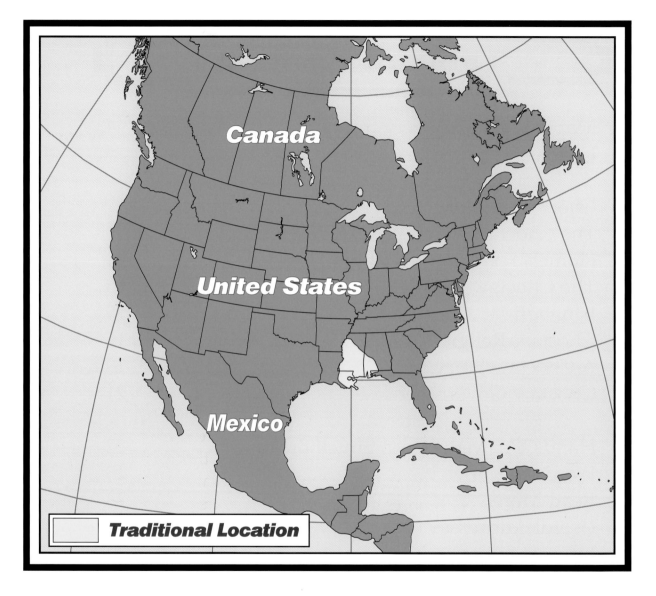

Traditional Location: Long ago, the Choctaws lived in the region that is now Mississippi, Louisiana, and Alabama.

Fast Facts

Today, the Choctaws are divided into several groups throughout the United States. The two largest groups are the Choctaw Nation of Oklahoma and the Mississippi Band of Choctaw Indians. These facts tell about the Choctaws in the past and the present.

Homes: Long ago, Choctaws lived in circular thatch lodges. Today, most Choctaws live in houses and apartments.

Food: Early Choctaws were farmers. They grew corn and squash. Choctaw men hunted wild game such as deer, bears, and rabbits. Women gathered nuts, berries, and wild fruits, including crabapples and grapes. Choctaws also caught trout and other fish.

Clothing: Early Choctaws wore clothing made from animal skins. Men dressed in leggings. Women wore skirts. Later, the Choctaws made clothing from cloth. They decorated their clothes with bright ribbons and beads. The Choctaws wear clothing like that of other North Americans today.

Language: The Choctaw language is a Western Muskogean language. Tribes who lived in the southeastern United States spoke Muskogean languages.

CHOCTAW WAR MEMORIAL

IN HONOR OF THOSE CHOCTAWS WHO
GAVE THEIR LIVES IN DEFENSE OF OUR NATION

THIS MEMORIAL IS DEDICATED TO THE ORIGINAL CHOCTAW CODE TALKERS OF WWI

JOSEPH OKLAHOMBI · BEN CARTERBY · WALTER VEACH · ALBERT BILLY · BEN HAMPTON
(THE MOST HIGHLY DECORATED WWI VETERAN IN OKLAHOMA) · ROBERT TAYLOR · JEFF NELSON · CALVIN WILSON · VICTOR BROWN
MITCHELL BOBB · PETE MAYTUBBY · SOLOMON LOUIS · JAMES EDWARDS · TOBIAS FRAZIER
JOSEPH DAVENPORT · GEORGE DAVENPORT · NOEL JOHNSON · OTIS LEADER

Choctaw Code Talkers

During World War I (1914–1918), 18 Choctaws served as soldiers in the U.S. Army. They spoke Choctaw when they gave information to other soldiers on the radio. The enemies heard the Choctaws, but they could not understand the language. The Choctaw soldiers became known as code talkers. They helped the United States and its allies win the war. The Choctaw War Memorial at the tribal Capitol Grounds in Tushka Homma, Oklahoma, honors the code talkers.

Choctaw History

Long ago, the Choctaws farmed peacefully in villages. The Choctaw Nation was one of the largest tribes in what is now the southeastern United States. More than 20,000 Choctaws lived in about 100 villages.

In 1540, Spanish explorer Hernando de Soto came to the Southeast looking for gold. He treated the Choctaws badly. Choctaw Chief Tuscaloosa and other Choctaws fought a battle with de Soto and his men. De Soto's men burned the Choctaw village of Mabila. Hundreds of people died.

European settlers came to Choctaw lands about 200 years later. The Choctaws were friendly to these colonists. The Choctaws helped the colonists fight the Revolutionary War (1775–1783) against England.

In the 1830s, the U.S. government took land from the Choctaws and many other tribes. The Choctaws were the first tribe forced to move to Oklahoma. U.S. soldiers made the Choctaws walk. Many people died. This long journey became known as the Trail of Tears.

The Choctaw People

Long ago, the Choctaws called themselves Okla Chahta. Okla is the Choctaw word for people. Spanish explorers used the name Chahta. This name refers to the custom of flattening babies' foreheads. A flat forehead was a sign of beauty to the Choctaw.

The Choctaws respected people who could speak well. When someone wanted to speak, the Choctaws built a brush structure with a hole in the roof. The speaker stood under the hole while speaking. The people sat in the shade of the structure. They would listen as long as the speaker could stand in the hot sun.

The Choctaws began to speak English as settlers came to their lands. Fewer Choctaws spoke the Choctaw language. Today, young Choctaws want to learn their traditional language. Schools offer Choctaw language classes. Choctaw elders sometimes teach the language. Some teachers give Choctaw language classes on the Internet.

Choctaw children study the Choctaw language in school.

Homes, Food, and Clothing

In the past, the Choctaws lived in circular lodges called hogans. They built a frame of strong poles tied together with vines. They put strips of cane between the poles and covered the cane with mud. Finally, they covered the mud and roof with thatch. Today, most Choctaws live in houses and apartments.

Much of the Choctaw's food came from forests. They ate berries, nuts, and fruits. Men hunted deer, bears, and other animals. Women grew vegetables such as corn, beans, pumpkins, and squash. Tanchi labona was a common Choctaw dish made with hominy, corn, and pork. Today, Choctaws buy food in grocery stores.

The early Choctaws made their clothing from animal hides. They decorated their clothing with bright beads and ribbons. Today, Choctaws wear modern clothing. But during festivals, women wear bright, colorful dresses. Men wear colorful shirts, belts trimmed with ribbon, and black hats.

At festivals, Choctaws wear bright clothing trimmed with ribbons.

The Choctaw Family

In the past, Choctaw families lived together in their hogans. Many members of the same family lived in one hogan. The women were in charge of cooking, planting, and taking care of the crops. Men hunted, fished, and made weapons.

Family members taught children the Choctaw way of life. A child's uncle helped to raise the child. Grandparents taught the children stories and played games with them. Mothers taught girls to tend the fields and to cook. Boys learned to hunt and to make weapons such as a blowgun. Boys blew darts through these hollow pieces of cane. Choctaw children had a lot of freedom.

When children were born, they were named after animals or an event at the time of their birth. Later, each child received a new name. This name told about a special honor or an adventure the child had. The Choctaw held special celebrations when children received a second name.

Today, Choctaw families take part in many traditional activities.

Ishtaboli

The Choctaws enjoyed playing games. Their favorite game was ishtaboli, or stickball. The Choctaws still play this rough sport today.

Two teams play on a long field with a goalpost at each end. Players use long sticks called kapuchas. Each stick has a webbed pocket at one end. Players use two kapuchas to throw and catch a small leather ball. They score by hitting a goalpost with the ball. Players can do almost anything to keep the other team from scoring. They may tackle other players. But they cannot touch the ball with their hands.

In the past, an ishtaboli game was an important event. Runners announced the game to other villages. People came from far away and camped around the field. The players painted their bodies with bright colors and hung animal tails from their belts. Each team had a medicine man. He stood beside a goalpost during the game to bring good luck to the players.

Choctaws play the traditional game of ishtaboli. The modern game of lacrosse came from ishtaboli.

Choctaw Religion

Long ago, the Choctaws believed that each person had an inner and an outer spirit. The inner spirit was called shilup. The outer spirit was called shilombish.

When a person died, the shilup traveled to the "Happy Land." The shilombish stayed at home until the funeral. Then it faded away. The shilombish would stay for a long time if the person had been bad. Today, the word shilup means "ghost." The word shilombish means "soul."

The Choctaws gave up many of their beliefs when they were moved to Oklahoma in the 1830s. Christian missionaries taught their religion to the Choctaws. The Choctaws accepted Christianity because the missionaries could provide education. Christianity is a religion that follows the teachings of Jesus Christ.

Today, most Choctaws believe in Christianity. But they still tell the old stories to remember the beliefs of their ancestors.

In 2000, Chief Gregory E. Pyle spoke at the dedication of the chapel in the newly built Choctaw Nation Hospital.

The Choctaws found Nanih Waiya in what is now Mississippi.

A Choctaw Story

Nanih Waiya is a low hill near Philadelphia, Mississippi. This mound is sacred to the Choctaws. They have many stories about Nanih Waiya. Choctaws from around the world visit the sacred mound. They tell their children the old stories.

One story says that long ago, the Choctaws did not have a home. They came from far in the northwest. Their holy men said that good land and good hunting were in the east. Chahta, their leader, carried a sacred pole on the journey to the new land. This pole would tell them which direction to travel.

Each night, Chahta stuck the pole into the ground. The next morning, the pole leaned to the east. The Choctaws followed the pole. Every day the pole pointed east. The journey was very long.

One day they reached a hill. In the morning, the pole was sticking straight up. Chahta said, "Here is where we shall live."

Choctaw Government

In the past, Choctaw lands were divided into three districts. A district chief was in charge of all the villages in a district. He was an honored and respected member of the tribe. Each village had a town chief and a war chief. Town chiefs took care of the village. War chiefs were in charge of battles.

A district chief called meetings. Chiefs from each village came to the meeting. They made laws and discussed tribal matters. They sometimes settled arguments. If the tribe had problems, the three district chiefs met to decide what to do.

Today, the Choctaw Nation has a tribal council with 12 members. The Choctaw Nation also has a chief and an assistant chief. Each council member and the chief are elected to four-year terms. The chief and council appoint the assistant chief. The chief and council make decisions about how to help the tribe.

The tribal council meets with the chief and program directors in the Choctaw Nation Administrative Complex in Oklahoma.

Hands On: Make Corn Shuck Bread

The Choctaw grew corn in their villages. They made corn shuck bread, or Banaha, from cornmeal. Ask an adult to help you cook this recipe.

What You Need

Water
Large pot
Measuring cups and spoons
6 cups corn meal
2 teaspoons baking soda

Medium bowl
Corn shucks
Shallow pan
Large spoon

What You Do

1. Fill a large pot with water. Heat the water until it boils.
2. Mix 6 cups corn meal and 2 teaspoons baking soda in a bowl. Carefully pour some of the boiling water over the mixture. It should make a soft dough. When the dough has cooled, knead the dough with your hands.
3. Put the corn shucks in a shallow pan. Soften them by carefully pouring some boiling water over them. When the softened shucks are cool, tear a few strips off of them.
4. Make a 1-inch (2.5-centimeter) dough ball and lay it on one shuck. Fold the shuck around the dough ball. Tie it together with the strips.
5. Carefully drop the wrapped dough balls into the pot of boiling water. Let them cook for 30 to 45 minutes.
6. Carefully remove the balls from the water with a spoon. Take the corn shucks off the bread. Serve bread alone or with a meal.

Words to Know

cane (CAYN)—a plant or grass that has a hollow, woody stem
colonist (KOL-uh-nist)—a person who lives in a colony; American colonists fought for freedom from England in the Revolutionary War (1775-1783).
council (KOUN-suhl)—a group of leaders
hominy (HOHM-i-nee)—corn kernels with the hulls removed
knead (NEED)—to press, fold, and stretch dough to make it smooth
missionary (MISH-uh-nair-ee)—a person who teaches a certain religion to a group of people
religion (ri-LIJ-uhn)—a set of spiritual beliefs people follow
shuck (SHUCK)—the outer casing of corn
thatch (THATCH)—a roofing made of straw, leaves, or grasses
tradition (truh-DISH-uhn)—a custom, an idea, or a belief that is handed down from one generation to the next

Read More

Ansary, Mir Tamim. *Southeast Indians.* Native Americans. Des Plaines, Ill.: Heinemann Library, 2000.
Girod, Christina M. *Native Americans of the Southeast.* Indigenous Peoples of North America. San Diego: Lucent Books, 2001.
Sherrow, Victoria. *The Choctaw.* Native American People. Vero Beach, Fla.: Rourke, 1997.

Useful Addresses

Choctaw Nation of Oklahoma
P.O. Drawer 1210
Durant, OK 74702

Nanih Waiya Historic Site
4496 Highway 393
Louisville, MS 39339

Mississippi Band of Choctaw
P.O. Box 6010
Highway 16 West
Choctaw Branch
Philadelphia, MS 39350

Internet Sites

Choctaw Music and Arts
http://cyberfair.gsn.org/bces/index.htm
Choctaw Nation of Oklahoma—Official Home Page
http://www.choctawnation.com
The Mississippi Band of Choctaw Indians
http://www.choctaw.org

Index